Your notes and drawings ↑↑↑

Your notes and drawings ↑↑↑

Your notes and drawings ↑↑↑

Your notes and drawings ↑↑↑

Your notes and drawings ↑↑↑

Your notes and drawings ↑↑↑

Your notes and drawings ↑↑↑

Your notes and drawings ↑↑↑

Your notes and drawings ↑↑↑

Your notes and drawings ↑↑↑

Your notes and drawings ↑↑↑

Your notes and drawings ↑↑↑

Your notes and drawings ↑↑↑

Your notes and drawings ↑↑↑

Your notes and drawings ↑↑↑

Your notes and drawings ↑↑↑

Your notes and drawings ↑↑↑

Your notes and drawings ↑↑↑

Your notes and drawings ↑↑↑

Your notes and drawings ↑↑↑

Your notes and drawings ↑↑↑

Your notes and drawings ↑↑↑

Your notes and drawings ↑↑↑

Your notes and drawings ↑↑↑

Your notes and drawings ↑↑↑

Your notes and drawings ↑↑↑

Your notes and drawings ↑↑↑

Your notes and drawings ↑↑↑

Your notes and drawings ↑↑↑

Your notes and drawings ↑↑↑

Your notes and drawings ↑↑↑

Your notes and drawings ↑↑↑

Your notes and drawings ↑↑↑

Your notes and drawings ↑↑↑

Your notes and drawings ↑↑↑

Your notes and drawings ↑↑↑

Your notes and drawings ↑↑↑

Your notes and drawings ↑↑↑

Your notes and drawings ↑↑↑

Your notes and drawings ↑↑↑

Your notes and drawings ↑↑↑

Your notes and drawings ↑↑↑

Your notes and drawings ↑↑↑

Your notes and drawings ↑↑↑

Your notes and drawings ↑↑↑

Your notes and drawings ↑↑↑

Your notes and drawings ↑↑↑

Your notes and drawings ↑↑↑

Your notes and drawings ↑↑↑

Your notes and drawings ↑↑↑

Your notes and drawings ↑↑↑

Your notes and drawings ↑↑↑

Your notes and drawings ↑↑↑

Your notes and drawings ↑↑↑

Your notes and drawings ↑↑↑

Your notes and drawings ↑↑↑

Your notes and drawings ↑↑↑

Your notes and drawings ↑↑↑

Your notes and drawings ↑↑↑

Your notes and drawings ↑↑↑

Your notes and drawings ↑↑↑

Your notes and drawings ↑↑↑

Your notes and drawings ↑↑↑

Your notes and drawings ↑↑↑

Your notes and drawings ↑↑↑

Your notes and drawings ↑↑↑

Your notes and drawings ↑↑↑

Your notes and drawings ↑↑↑

Your notes and drawings ↑↑↑

Your notes and drawings ↑↑↑

Your notes and drawings ↑↑↑

Your notes and drawings ↑↑↑

Your notes and drawings ↑↑↑

Your notes and drawings ↑↑↑

Your notes and drawings ↑↑↑

Your notes and drawings ↑↑↑

Your notes and drawings ↑↑↑

Your notes and drawings ↑↑↑

Your notes and drawings ↑↑↑

Your notes and drawings ↑↑↑

Your notes and drawings ↑↑↑

Your notes and drawings ↑↑↑

Your notes and drawings ↑↑↑

Your notes and drawings ↑↑↑

Your notes and drawings ↑↑↑

Your notes and drawings ↑↑↑

Your notes and drawings ↑↑↑

Your notes and drawings ↑↑↑

Your notes and drawings ↑↑↑

Your notes and drawings ↑↑↑

Your notes and drawings ↑↑↑

Your notes and drawings ↑↑↑

Your notes and drawings ↑↑↑

Your notes and drawings ↑↑↑

Your notes and drawings ↑↑↑

Your notes and drawings ↑↑↑

Your notes and drawings ↑↑↑

Printed in Poland
by Amazon Fulfillment
Poland Sp. z o.o., Wrocław